How to Get Divorced

The Ultimate Guide to the Divorce Process and Advice for an Amicable Divorce

by Lindy McIntyre

Table of Contents

Introduction

Divorce can make you feel like your entire world is falling apart. While going through such a challenging and painful experience, most ex-spouses find it difficult to get along. However, it is definitely possible for the process of divorce to go more smoothly for both parties. There is indeed a way to avoid the draining arguments, tedious squabbling and endless headaches. Whether or not prenuptial agreements were in place, there is hope to make divorce as painless as possible.

Divorce is difficult enough without the extreme life changes that can occur after you split with your spouse. So, it's important to maintain some semblance of a normal life, keeping a sense of security as much as possible. To help maximize that sense of normalcy, be sure to divide marital property in a fair manner. For example, if your parents left you an inheritance, or you attained property or money from a previous marriage, make sure that remains intact. This is especially important if you have children and want to protect those assets for their future.

You'll need a divorce lawyer to make sure you don't get the short end of the stick. The attorney will ensure that what you get or keep from the deal is fair and reasonable. In any case, in a contested divorce, the court will require both parties to obtain a lawyer.

Contested divorce, uncontested divorce, mediation separation and so on.... What do they all mean? This book will briefly yet thoroughly cover all of these terms in the pages to come. By the time you finish reading, you will have gained a complete understanding of the divorce process and how to make it as smooth and painless as possible.

Be encouraged. You are not the only couple going through this process. 50% of first marriages end in divorce, and 65% of second marriages end in divorce. So, don't feel defeated or guilty if your marriage isn't working out. Look at this as an opportunity to start a new and exciting chapter in your life. Just be sure you know how to handle the process to make it as easy and pain-free as you can.

Chapter 1: Identifying the Grounds for Divorce, and Being Sure It's What You Want

Divorce is full of mixed emotions and difficult decisions. It's the hardest, and most complicated, when it involves kids or property acquired together. That said, divorce happens every day and the minute you decide to get a divorce, factors such as the prenuptial agreement and child support should be immediately considered.

First things first, you need to identify the grounds for divorce. As both you and your spouse know, it did not simply happen overnight. There is at least one solid reason behind the decision to split.

Here are some of the reasons considered valid enough to nullify your marriage:

1. Adultery

If your spouse had sexual relations with someone else other than yourself, it is only natural that you resent them for betraying your trust. This is a valid ground for divorce but there is a catch. It is only valid if you file for a divorce right away. If you don't file for divorce, and continue to live with your spouse for months after you found out they were committing adultery, then this reason becomes invalid.

2. Desertion

If your spouse has left you without any valid reason or your consent for more than two years, then it is grounds for divorce. If your spouse decides to simply end the marriage without your agreement, you have the right to file for divorce.

3. Separation for More Than 2 Years

If you and your spouse have lived apart for more than 2 years, you can mutually agree to get divorced. This must be done in writing, detailing every legal aspect. If you have been separated for more than 5 years, then you have sufficient grounds for a divorce even if your spouse does not agree.

4. Unreasonable Behavior

If your spouse has exhibited some unreasonable behavior that are unchanging and beyond your control, then you have enough ground to file for divorce. Unreasonable behavior could include:

- Drug abuse and alcoholism

- Physical violence

- Failure of provision in housekeeping

- Verbal abuse such as threats or insults

Chapter 2: Legal Requirements for Divorce

If you are thinking of getting a divorce, it is important to equip yourself with the necessary legal requirements in your state or county. This will play a big role in outlining and establishing your case. In addition, this information helps you save time and resources.

Note that many states observe a policy known as "no-fault divorce". This means that the court doesn't take into consideration who is at fault for the ended marriage. So, since legal requirements for divorce vary in each state and county, make sure you consult with your lawyer about the current requirements.

In normal situations, divorce cases are settled in court and there is usually the policy of 'no-fault divorce.' Again, this means that the courts don't care which spouse was to blame for the marital annulment.

Here are some of the legal requirements that must be taken into account before filing for divorce:

1. Residency

The party filing for marriage annulment must have been a resident of the state for no less than 3 months prior to filing for a divorce.

2. Legal Grounds

When you boil it down, there are only two types of legal reasons for divorce. One is incurable insanity, and the other is irreconcilable differences. In the case of irreconcilable differences, it means that both parties are not in a position to solve the accumulated difficulties that have led to the breakdown of the marriage.

3. Waiting Period

The waiting period is the duration that both parties are required to wait for the court to validate their divorce. Neither party is allowed to re-marry during this waiting process. Note that the waiting period is usually from 0-12 months and 6 months on average.

4. Jurisdictional Requirement

This means that the marriage annulment must be handled in the correct court, which is in the county that either spouse has resided for no less than 3 months prior to the divorce process.

Chapter 3: Preparing Your Children for Divorce

Considering that marriage annulment is already a bombshell to the two spouses involved, you can imagine how overwhelming it can be for the children. During the divorce process, children are bound to get lost and confused. In most cases the parents fail to shield their children from the drama that comes with the divorce process. Children are fragile and not quite old enough to understand why their parents are splitting up.

Naturally, children are bound to get upset and in some instances blame themselves for the divorce. In turn, this can cause friction and anxiety between parents and children. Some children may experience withdrawal symptoms and poor academic performance. This may also cause social problems, acting out or also withdrawing from friends. It is therefore your duty as parents to assure your children that they will safe, loved and protected during the whole process.

For the sake of your kids, don't drag them through the painful process. Keep all the arguments and hard decisions away from them. Each parent should take extra time and effort to express how love and care for their children. With time, the children will wrap their heads around the process and adjust to the changes.

In the case of older children, you might want to sit down and have an open, honest conversation with them. Make sure you listen to them well and allow them to express their emotions. Assure them that, no matter what happens, you and your spouse will always be there for them even after splitting. Do not expect your children to embrace the news overnight. Give them space and allow them to take it all in at their own pace.

Children will react differently to the news of a divorce depending on their age, disposition and the circumstances leading up to the ended marriage. Here are some tips that you can use to help your children cope with the divorce process:

- Each parent should be sure to remain a strong presence in the child's life

- The 'blame game' and negativity should be kept far from your child's ears

- Try to minimize the effect of the divorce on your child's daily routine

Chapter 4: How to Divorce Without Ruining Your Life

As it is, divorce can be an ugly and emotional process that easily consumes both parties and causes high drama. However, it doesn't have to be quite so extreme, not if you approach it in a loving and thoughtful way. By the time a marriage ends, both parties usually see it coming. This gives you time to create a sense of mutuality between you and your spouse.

Use a friendly tone when addressing your spouse and they will be more likely to respond in the same way. Keep your sense of self-respect, and respect for your spouse even as you part ways. If you feel that things become overly intense, you can try to seek common ground.

Invest in a professional therapist to help you handle the trauma that comes with divorce. Once a marriage comes to end, you are bound to feel low self-esteem and emotions such as rejection and hopelessness can be triggered. A therapist should be in a position to help you work through these emotions without being judgmental. Also, don't be afraid to seek out help from friends and loved ones. They can provide compassion and love during such a difficult time.

Get a good lawyer who will advise you on important matters such as child custody, division of wealth, support/alimony and how to handle the prenuptial agreement. Basically, your lawyer should play the role of litigator, strategist, negotiator and problem solver. Ask among friends, colleagues and family to find a competent divorce lawyer.

It is key to avoid playing dirty, especially as far as division of wealth is concerned. Hiding any assets accumulated during the marriage is a big no-no. This might land you in trouble and possibly end up ruining your life.

Try to resolve your issues through divorce mediation so you can avoid a divorce court. Research indicates that spouses who resolve their conflicts outside a divorce court are more likely to have an amicable dissolution of their marriage.

Chapter 5: Uncontested Divorce

If you decide to go through the 'pro se' route, make sure that both you and your spouse are emotionally detached and rational enough to get through any differences or difficult issues without argument.

Contrary to popular belief, an uncontested divorce does not automatically translate to embracing the terms and conditions one-hundred percent. It means that both parties have to mutually agree to live with the set terms and conditions.

Uncontested divorce is viewed as the easiest and the cheapest way of getting a divorce. If you and your spouse intend to maintain a relationship with mutual respect after the process, go the uncontested way. If you have budget concerns, the uncontested divorce will be especially good since you won't have to worry about attorney fees.

Here are some other reasons you might want to go the uncontested route:

- **It provides privacy and confidentiality**

An uncontested divorce ensures privacy and confidentiality during the divorce process. Considering that it can be headache enough, having your business out there for all to see can worsen the process.

- **It is the amicable option**

If you and your spouse intend to maintain a cordial relationship after the divorce, then an uncontested divorce will be a good start. The fact that you and your spouse will negotiate and arrive at a middle ground on various matters will set the stage for a tension-free relationship. This also creates an avenue for forgiveness and healing in the future. An uncontested divorce will minimize the drama as it provides a platform for both of you to have a say in key decisions involving child custody, alimony and wealth division.

- **It is faster and quicker**

As you can imagine, the divorce process not only consumes your emotions, but your time and energy as well. It is therefore natural that you would want the faster, easier option. An uncontested divorce is a speedy process, allowing you all the more time to adjust, recover and mend from a failed marriage.

Note that if you decide to represent yourself as a pro se litigant, you may face some form of resistance from your spouse's attorney. Know that the court is not obliged to offer you immunity as you work your way through the procedures of civil practice.

Chapter 6: Contested Divorce

Ideally every couple would choose an uncontested divorce, but things can sometimes get too out of hand for that option. No matter how hard you try to achieve a common ground with your estranged spouse, it's not always possible. When it gets to the point where you cannot agree on terms, a contested divorce becomes the only way out.

Some of the unresolved issues that could lead to a contested divorce are disagreements regarding; wealth division, alimony/spousal support, child support and visitation. In the case of a contested divorce, both you and your spouse must file court documents. These court documents explain your positions and the source(s) of dispute.

Once you file the documents, you will be issued a case management process that will offer both of you scheduled opportunities to outline your dispute. The main agenda of case management is to ensure that both of you are in a position to settle as fast as possible without consuming too much time and money.

In most cases, your dispute will be resolved in confined rooms prior to the case hearing. In some instances, a case may be resolved sooner than expected, even before the trial.

Unlike an uncontested divorce, a contested one is usually drawn out and the duration of the entire process depends on when the case is resolved. At times, the case may not be resolved easily and drag out even more.

Note that if the case is not settled before trial, a judge has the mandate to finalize the case and grant a divorce. Usually, the divorce is deemed final 31 days after it is granted.

As mentioned earlier, it is possible that you and your spouse come to a mutual agreement before the actual trial. This is referred to as a settlement. Usually, a settlement cannot be appealed as it is assumed both of you are happy with your decision. An agreement usually marks a halt to litigation as it is deemed final.

Chapter 7: A Prenuptial Agreement Makes Things Better

It is entirely up to each couple whether they choose to draw up a prenuptial agreement or not. Of course, the terms of a prenuptial agreement vary from one couple to the next. While some dismiss the idea of a premarital agreement, deeming it 'unromantic', the agreement is actually a good idea for most married couples. It doesn't mean the marriage is sentenced to failure from the start, it's simply a back-up for 'just in case'.

A prenuptial agreement could erase many problems that might arise in the unfortunate event of a divorce. Here are some of the benefits associated with a prenuptial arrangement:

- Makes it easier for you and your spouse to separate individual finances and establish the wealth accumulated during marriage as either community or marital property. In the event of a divorce or demise of one spouse, community or marital property is fairly divided between the parties as agreed in the prenuptial agreement.

- Saves both spouses from unnecessary debts especially debts accumulated prior to the marriage. A prenuptial agreement protects you from malicious creditors who might use this opportunity to exploit your situation. More so, a prenuptial agreement limits your liability for the debts accrued by your spouse.

- Defines what share each party should get in case of a divorce. A prenuptial arrangement plays a huge role in establishing rules as far as wealth division is concerned and this can minimize drama during the divorce process.

- A prenuptial arrangement outlines the provision for children from previous relationships.

- A prenuptial arrangement clarifies responsibility in the course of marriage.

With these points in mind, you will find no need to view a prenuptial agreement in a negative light. It is actually quite advantageous to both you and your partner. Look at a prenuptial arrangement as an agreement that will protect you and your spouse during marriage and in the event of a divorce.

Whether the marriage works out or not, the agreement makes it easier to plan for the future.

Chapter 8: Why You Need a Divorce Attorney

When your marriage is falling apart and divorce is inevitable, seeking a family attorney is advisable. It might seem convenient to represent yourself in court; using documents and ideas from books or online sources. However, it is important to have somebody who understands the basics and the depths of law regarding the divorce process. They will represent your interests and shorten the litigation case.

There are many solid reasons to hire a divorce lawyer. To start, an experienced attorney is your gateway to a successful divorce settlement. If you have complicated issues regarding assets and properties, it is even more important to use a lawyer.

Matters involving assets often result into conflicts. Add the highly sensitive emotional state to these conflicts and it can seem an impossible task to solve any issue. This is where the divorce attorney comes to the rescue, able to articulate each side in a skillful and impartial/reasonable manner.

Secondly, the divorce procedure is very complex. It even becomes more complicated, with the stress that comes with the whole ordeal. There are papers to file, court proceedings to attend, difficult decisions to make and numerous other tasks to execute.

Considering that you are in the emotional process of divorcing your life partner, you are bound to make mistakes. This is where a divorce attorney comes in handy.

Family lawyers also ensure that all the legal documents are presented to the courts in time and in a straightforward, organized way. They make sure that, as their client, your interests are well represented. On top of that, they know how to avoid unforeseen delays.

Divorce courts work with deadlines. Failure to comply with these set time schedules can be a costly mistake. Divorce attorneys ensure that the case takes the shortest amount of time possible. Lastly, a divorce lawyer takes care of everything and leaves you the time and energy to deal with the emotional side of the divorce.

Chapter 9: Separation Agreement

A separation agreement is a legally binding agreement between two parties who have decided to live separately. Note that this is that it is an *agreement*, requiring the couple to consent to a mutual set of terms.

Usually the agreement is tailored to settle alimony, property, debt, visitation, child custody, child support and insurance issues. These issues show up in almost every separation agreement. However, each agreement is unique and can include other aspects.

To collaborate smoothly on the separation agreement, people use different methods. Mediation is helpful to bring two spouses together to resolve their disputes. Note that this is not the same as marriage counseling. Mediation is not geared towards reconciling the couple, but rather enabling them to solve their conflicts out of court.

Each spouse can also write their own separation agreement. In this case, it is essential that each spouse hires their own solicitor.

Another method to come up with a separation agreement is through collaborative practice. Both parties collaborate to find solutions for various matters regarding their separation. You will definitely need lawyers to steer this process. After the terms of agreement are clear, a deed of separation is created.

The legally binding 'separation agreement' contract consists of the following elements:

- An agreement to go separate ways

- Arrangements in relation to child custody and visitation rights

- Ownership and occupation of the matrimonial home and other properties

- Maintenance and other lump sum payments

- Guaranteed protection from debts incurred by the other spouse

- Succession rights

Separation agreement can save divorcing partners a lot of money and time. They just need to agree on various issues such as property division, child custody and support, insurance and so on. If you choose to divorce, you and your spouse should be prepared to cooperate until a deed of separation is drawn.

Chapter 10: Marital Division of Property

Marital property division is an integral aspect of the divorce procedure. It is mostly characterized by disagreements as each party feels they are entitled to more than the other.

The marital division of property does not include individual properties acquired before the union. In most cases and in particular where the parties do not have a prenuptial agreement, a 50-50 sharing rule applies.

What defines marital property? Any property titled under both names of the couple is deemed marital property. Again, this doesn't include gifts or assets acquired by a spouse before marriage. Nor does it include property acquired individually after legal separation.

In addition, if both parties agreed to exclude a certain asset from the pool of marital property, that is not considered either. A property that was given to one spouse by the other is likewise excluded during the division of marital property.

Although it is clear that the courts should follow the provisions of equitable property distribution, they only reach a settlement after considering a few things. They must establish the contribution of each party to the marital property. The courts will also take into account the value assigned to each party and the custodial requirements of the children if any.

Other aspects that will have an impact on the division include age, health, occupation, liabilities and needs of both parties. In addition, they will evaluate the possible outcomes of the marital division of property in the case of each spouse. As you can see, this cannot be handled on your own. To make the procedure smooth and bearable, find a divorce attorney.

Note that giving false information about your assets will be a costly mistake. It will prolong the case and the judges may be convinced to act in favor of your spouse. Be on the safe side and provide all necessary documents.

Chapter 11: Child Support and Visitation Rights in a Divorce

If a divorcing couple has children, child support and visitation become an often emotional part of the issues that will be discussed in court. Child support and visitation rights parallel each other and the judge will decide which is in the best interest of the child.

Keep in mind that that the court will not consider the prenup or any other document when making the decision. Instead, they listen to both sides and utilize the evidence forwarded to the court to make the most sensible decision.

Child support ensures that the child does not lack in anything until they are of legal age. It is the responsibility each parent to pay the child support. Regardless of whether you are the custodial parent or not, it is a legal offence not to pay the due child support.

The only time you can be excused is if you have already filed a motion to change the child support order owing to financial circumstances. Yet, you will have to keep paying the set amount until the court revokes the earlier order.

Defaulting on the payment of child support can have serious consequences. Usually, once the court establishes that you no longer pay your child support allocation the following things may happen:

- Cancellation of your driver's license

- Denial of any professional license

- Being denied state grants and loans

- Imprisonment

Now, visitation rights are a different matter. They allow the non-custodial parent to freely see the child. These rights are extremely good for the child. It makes them feel that even if their parents are apart, they still care and are a part of the child's life.

Visitation rights designate the times that the visiting parent sees the child. Whoever gets the child access rights must adhere to the guidelines given in the order. If they fail to comply with the conditions, the court may withdraw the rights.

Divorce courts in many states put the interest of the child at top priority. They are make sure to follow up on whether the divorced parties are adhering to the orders.

Chapter 12: The Role of Mediation in Divorce

As divorce rate is now higher than ever, family courts have adopted the use of other tools to make the process short and stress-free. One such strategy is mediation, which is used to enable two parties to solve issues such as child support, alimony, property division and so forth.

Its main goal is to give the couple an opportunity to settle their differences the best way they can. This will rule out the need for the judges to make decisions regarding the issues on their behalf.

Mediation is encouraged in several states, particularly in cases that concern children. The process is steered by a divorce mediator who helps the couple to come up with agreeable solutions.

Note that the mediator only acts as a neutral party. They do not represent either party or offer legal advice. A mediator will not represent you in the courtroom afterwards. You will need a divorce attorney for that.

Mediation discusses the restraining orders, child support, custody, paternity issues and visitation. Yet, not everybody is a candidate for the mediation process. If you cannot communicate with the other partner appropriately, it will be impossible to employ this strategy. Both parties must be willing to collaborate with each other to settle property division, child support, alimony, and joint-debt settlement plan.

Mediation has added benefits. For one, it is less expensive than a divorce lawyer, helping prevent a lengthy divorce process in a bid to solve the related issues. Secondly, it keeps sensitive matters as discreet as possible instead of taking them to the courtrooms. Mediation also protects children from hearing their parents argue in court.

Where children are involved, mediation is the best approach. It ensures that the interests of each party are considered in a peaceful manner. The courts will only decide on matters related to child custody. Mediation is an effective way of reducing conflicts in divorce.

Chapter 13: Collaborative Divorce

Collaborative divorce is a new, yet popular approach in family law. It calls for both parties to hire their own collaborative divorce lawyer, who will help them in negotiating an agreement on various issues. If an agreement is not reached, then the attorneys will have to withdraw. Keep in mind that, once the collaborative divorce starts, the lawyers you hired cannot represent you in a contested legal case.

The best aspect of the collaborative divorce procedure is that it protects confidentiality and privacy. It also gives both parties an opportunity to reach an agreement without going to court. Although the process involves a significant number of people, it requires complete cooperation. You must be ready to use honesty and reason.

One big reason to choose collaborative divorce is that both parties are offered legal support. The lawyers represent the interests of each spouse. They help clarify the issues put forward by the other party. In addition, other trained professionals come to your assistance to help reach agreeable solutions. An added bonus is that spouses are able to make informed decisions.

All disputes between spouses are meant to be resolved in a respectful manner in a collaborative divorce. It ensures that the parties do not part with any unresolved conflicts pending. Where there are children, this procedure can protect the kids from emotional pain. Sometimes, court proceedings regarding child support, marital property division and alimony can get heated up in the courtrooms. It is healthier that your children not see this tug of war between spouses.

Finally, if you take matters in an open court, you will have to give all the details in relation to your properties, the grounds for divorce and any other matter that needs to be placed before the court. If you want to avoid a public display of all these sensitive matters, consider applying for a collaborative divorce.

Chapter 14: Don't Start Dating Until the Case Is Finally Settled

You may feel the desire to start dating during the divorce. It's fairly common and understandable to long for someone to replace the emptiness and sadness you experience while separating. It's nice and convenient to have a new romantic partner to help you through this emotionally vulnerable time. As appealing as it may seem, it's wise to not act on this desire. Try your best to keep from starting a new relationship until the divorce case is finalized. There are a number of reasons to refrain from dating as you await the final settling of your divorce case.

First, your marriage remains legally intact until the court orders you and your spouse's official separation. So, if your spouse finds out that you're dating, they will have enough cause to give you extra trouble in court. Even if your spouse has been unfaithful during the marriage, they will likely feel that you are not justified in dating someone else.

For the sake of the children, as well as yourself, you should keep good relations with your spouse. Dating will make it difficult to cooperate with them during the process. Aside from all these reasons, there are some legal repercussions as well.

The law still recognizes you as a married person. Dating during the divorce process is regarded as adultery. Such developments can affect the decision of the court on issues including eventual property settlement and spousal support. Even if you have been separated for a long time, dating will only add to the list of marital misconduct.

If you would like to be given the custody of the children, you must display the best conduct. If you are living with the person in your new relationship, it will decrease the amount of child support or alimony allocated to you. So, hold onto any impulse to date until you are officially granted a divorce. Your patience will pay off in the end, even if it seems difficult at the moment.

Conclusion

Ideally, all marriages would last happily ever after. But unfortunately, in reality many married couples don't have this happy, fairy tale ending. As stated earlier, statistics show that first time American marriages have just over a 50% chance of succeeding.

You would think that second marriages would last longer because the involved couples a more mature and have more experience. Yet, it only gets worse. Second marriages in America have a 65% chance of failing. And the regressing pattern continues with third marriages...it only gets harder to stay together.

When divorce is inevitable, as difficult as it might seem, you have to deal with the process. It may feel like your heart is breaking, but it really isn't the end of the world. It's simply a new beginning and a chance at a fresh start. You have to do what's ultimately best for you and your children. But, this doesn't mean that you have to let the divorce process take over and become this huge, dramatic ordeal. You can take control and take steps to ensure it goes as smoothly and agreeably as possible.

Hopefully this book has helped you, at least a little, to prepare for divorce. At least it will give you an overview of what's to come in the divorce process and show you the options. Remember, don't attempt to do this on your own - get a divorce attorney as well as support from family and friends.

Finally, I'd like to thank you for reading this book! If you found it helpful, I'd greatly appreciate it if you'd take a moment to leave a review on Amazon. Thank you!

Made in the USA
Middletown, DE
26 November 2022

16074773R00040